THE TRANS
OF

CW00506409

and the Subterranean Spheres of the Earth

SIGISMUND VON GLEICH

TEMPLE LODGE

Translated from German by Matthew Barton

Temple Lodge Publishing
Hillside House, The Square
Forest Row, RH18 5ES

www.templelodge.com

First published in English by Temple Lodge 2005

Originally published in German under the title *Die Umwandlung des Bösen* by J. Ch. Mellinger Verlag GmbH in 1983

© J. Ch. Mellinger Verlag GmbH 1983
This translation © Temple Lodge Publishing 2005

The moral right of the author has been asserted under the Copyright, Designs and Patents Act, 1988

All rights reserved. No part of this publication may be reproduced, stored in a retrieval system, or transmitted, in any form or by any means, electronic, mechanical, photocopying or otherwise, without the prior permission of the publishers

A catalogue record for this book is available from the British Library

ISBN 1 902636 71 6

Cover by Andrew Morgan
Typeset by DP Photosetting, Aylesbury, Bucks.
Printed and bound by Cromwell Press Limited, Trowbridge, Wilts.

Contents

Foreword

Sigismund von Gleich was born on Michaelmas Day (29 September) 1896 in Ludwigsburg, Germany as the second son of a German army officer. A career in the army was considered his birthright and destiny, but fate and von Gleich's own determination intervened. A short time after he began his military service he became ill with disease of the lungs. His mother, while visiting him at a clinic, met a woman who gave her a copy of Rudolf Steiner's book *Theosophy*, which she in turn gave to her son. This book changed his life. By the end of World War I he saw his life's task to become completely informed about and involved in anthroposophy. Such a course of action produced friction with and alienation from his father, who was a Catholic, a general in the army, and an opponent of Rudolf Steiner.

There were no 'jobs' in anthroposophy at that time where one could pursue a conventional path to success. However, von Gleich managed to find employment with Eugen Kolisko and Walter Johannes Stein. His first book appeared in 1922 and was titled *Von Thales bis Steiner* (From Thales to Steiner). He next worked for the publication *Die Drei* and became a public lecturer on behalf of anthroposophy. After the rise of National Socialism he moved to Zeist, Holland, with his wife and three children, where he continued his writing and lecturing. His four-volume major work *Marksteine der Kulturgeschichte* (Milestones in Cultural History) began appearing in 1938, the last volume of which was published at Easter 1953 and first appeared in English in 1997 with the title *The Sources of Inspiration of Anthroposophy*.[1] He died on All Saints Day (1 November) 1953 in Zeist at age 57.

The Transformation of Evil, published posthumously in 1954 as *Die Umwandlung des Bösen*, was developed from a series of three essays published in 1953 and appears here for the first time in English translation. Just as the topic of evil occupied von Gleich in the last months of his life, so it was a focus of Rudolf Steiner in the closing days of his life. Steiner's very last 'Leading Thought',[2] written only days before his death in March 1925, for the first time discussed the concept of sub-nature (the subsensible) and its relationship to mechanical forces and technology, the understanding of which is of critical importance for the future of human life and development on earth. This final 'Leading Thought' inspired von Gleich to pen these essays. Steiner was writing in 1925, when memories of the tragedy of 'The War to End All Wars' (World War I) were still fresh and painful. For von Gleich World War II was only eight years in the past, and the wartime devastation was still visible throughout much of continental Europe. The reality of human evil occupied them both in their last days on earth.

The Transformation of Evil is one of a handful of writings to offer insight into those realms situated below the surface of the earth which are described by Rudolf Steiner alternatively as the realm of sub-nature or the subterranean spheres. Its very title addresses the main issue head-on since, as von Gleich observes, 'the mysteries of evil ... are also those of the interior of the earth' (see page 27).

Von Gleich points to the importance of Rudolf Steiner's message about these domains, and acknowledges that both Steiner's groundbreaking work and his own contributions provide the germs of spiritual concepts and ideas which will require further elaboration and elucidation in the future.

It is fair to ask what relevance a 50-year-old, modestly-sized and relatively obscure book can have to conditions in the first years of the twenty-first century. What new insights into the nature and causes of evil could it offer?

The ideas put forth in this work have relevance to current economic, social and cultural conditions as evil, in its various guises, seems to be overwhelming humanity on all sides. For 'the civilized activities of humanity are gradually sliding downward, not only into the lowest regions of nature, but even *beneath nature*. Technical science and industry have become sub-nature'.[3]

The three essays comprising this work cover a lot of ground. The first essay 'Sub-nature or Tartarus' opens with a summary of the classical picture of the Underworld derived from Greek mythology. Next follows 'The Layers of the Interior of the Earth' where the various qualities and characteristics of each of the nine chthonic layers are set forth. The closing chapter entitled 'May the Power of Goodness Transform All Evil' briefly characterizes the polar counter-impulses of 'the good' (esoteric Christianity) to the nine currents of evil harboured in the earth's interior.

This work allows us to look upon the last 50 years of the twentieth century from both von Gleich's perspective, as for him they comprised the unknown future, and for ourselves, as they comprise our history and past. He makes the observation (page 58) that 'we are at the threshold of unimaginable advances' (of technology). We have the luxury of being able to see the further development and intensification of spiritual, scientific, economic and social trends which in von Gleich's time were in their infancy. The worlds of 'science and industry' have, indeed, descended more deeply into the sphere of sub-nature. Most technological advances (and some gigantic business enterprises) have been founded upon achievements in realms not visible to the senses: in sub-nature, the subsensible.

Technology and the ideal of 'progress though technology', promoted as an unalloyed 'good' in the early 1950s, is better understood in our time as a two-edged sword that can both bless and curse. Nuclear power and nuclear weapons technology, space exploration, laser beam technology, all that the silicon chip and digital technology have brought into daily life and the pending developments in biogenetics, neuropharmacology, gene therapy and nanotechnology[4] were on and over the cultural horizon in von Gleich's time.

We in 2005 are living at a time of enormously rapid change in information and communications technology. Technological advances have speeded up as the decades have passed by. The speed and density of computation power, which was doubling every three years at the beginning of the twentieth century, increased to a doubling every year by the end of the century.[5] The pending 'internet convergence', where all electronic devices will be 'internet enabled', will merge what formerly were separate technologies into one universal digital world which speaks the same language (the Internet Protocol), enabling intercommunication through wireless transmission. Previously distinct devices are already morphing into each other. These devices may look different on the outside, but on the inside they will become more and more alike. Telephones can function like TVs, cameras or laptops and receive both photos, videos, music, text messages and emails. Your laptop can play music on compact disks (cds), movies on digital versatile disks (dvds), receive both as streaming data or as downloads, function as sophisticated calculating, computing, graphics, design and word-processing machines, speak to other computers, your camera, Palm Pilot, iPod, Blackberry, telephone, home entertainment centre, refrigerator, security system, lighting systems, garage door ... you name it. Further, all this can be accomplished with high-speed wireless connections. There soon will be no need to have a physical dial-up or cable connection to the internet as buildings, shopping centres, even entire cities will be wired to transmit bits of digital data.

Computer chips are already being implanted into pets, executives, criminals and some children to track their location. The connection between computers and the human brain grows closer each year, as science is in the process of creating 'hybrid computers' based on biological systems, where the electrical impulses in the brain connect to electrical impulses flowing through the silicon chip. Scientists ask 'another critical question for understanding the twenty-first century: can an intelligence create another intelligence more intelligent that itself?'[6] Machines (computers) are now creating their own children—other computers. Intelligence itself, when detached from its source, offers dangers we can only imagine. Thus, the 'magical' nature of technology which von Gleich speaks of (page 58) is omnipresent. So, too, is the 'super-technology' (page 13) which is founded upon a 'super-materialism'[7] predicted by Steiner in the 1920s. 'Super-materialism', and its manifestation in 'super-technology', 'comes to be viewed as an autonomous process, having a life of its own that proceeds automatically, and almost naturally, along a singular path. Supposedly self-defining and independent of social power and purpose, technology appears to be an external force impinging upon society, as it were from outside, determining events to which people must forever adjust.'[8]

The dangers such technologies pose to human beings are manifold, personal privacy and security being only two areas of concern. Yet the blessings are also numerous and substantial. This Foreword is being written on a personal computer, which is linked to the internet and which

communicates with the folks at Temple Lodge Publishing—
on another continent—and with others worldwide, instan-
taneously, miraculously and at low cost. *Please don't take my
computer away! I can't live without it!*

*

The cultural decline since von Gleich's time is evident on all
sides. Cultural decadence and decay are openly discussed.
Pornography is ubiquitous and sexual stimulation by the
media is a given. Serial killers are no longer exceptional or
shocking. Rape, mutilation and cannibalism have become
standard techniques of war. Even mainstream psychoanalysis
concedes that everyone, and every group, is capable of the
most heinous acts. Genocide has become part of the modern
political landscape, as the Jewish Holocaust of World War II,
once thought to be a singular phenomenon, has been followed
by other genocides in Cambodia, Rwanda, and other wars of
mass murder (ethnic cleansing) in the former Yugoslavia, East
Timor, the Sudan and the Republic of Congo. Terrorism, once
limited to specific times and places, such as during the French
and Russian Revolutions, is now a worldwide phenomenon
used by various groups and governments to attain political
objectives not otherwise within their reach. These problems
have their source in human nature, in ourselves.

*

The ideas of Rudolf Steiner, summarized and further
developed by von Gleich in this book, are revolutionary in the
extreme. At their core they offer a new understanding of evil
and its role in human and divine evolution, a more profound
concept of the earth, and a more comprehensive picture of the
human being. Three principal concepts set forth in these
pages deserve emphasis.

First: the human being is pictured as standing between, and as a product of, the interworking of three realms: the super-sensible (super-nature), the sensible (nature) and the sub-sensible (sub-nature). This is critical to comprehending the modern path of knowledge, for 'sub-nature must be understood for what it really is. This can only be done properly *if we rise in spiritual knowledge at least as far into extra-terrestrial super-nature as we have descended in the techno-logical sciences into sub-nature*' (page 14). Those who have faulted anthroposophy for failing to have a 'shadow side' (Carl Jung) or for not dealing forthrightly with the dark side of human nature will find a rich harvest of ideas here.

Second: von Gleich cites a 'law of polarity' as an over-arching concept which applies not only to the manifestation of evil in the world, but which is a fundamental principal of creation itself, operating from the beginnings of our planetary system since its beginning on Old Saturn and continuing now through to its completion. The specific quote reads as follows:

> When one force begins to work in the universe another force, opposed to the first, arises at the same moment. Everything that happens in the world is subject to the law of polarity. Thus, to the degree that the free activity of the divine, the light, the creative and the good arise, at the same time there must also arise their counter-pole and sediment: the sub-earthly (hell), darkness, destruction and evil. [Page 35]

Finally, lest one goes too far overboard and falls into the trap of seeing the world simply in stark categories of good/evil, light/dark, creative/destructive, von Gleich reminds us that 'all sub-earthly counter-hierarchies were originally nothing other than the brothers, left behind, of beings who ascended upwards. And the fact that they remain in the earth's depths was initially a sacrifice on their part.' (Page 35.) Rudolf Steiner makes a similar point when he states: 'Thus in cosmic evolution it is the case that the gods themselves have called their opponents into being... So we see that we must not look for the origin of evil in the so-called "evil" beings, but in the "good" beings who, through their renunciation, first brought evil about through those beings who were able to bring it into the world.'[9]

It is hoped that the rich content of this small book may provide the stimulus for further work by others in this area.

Paul V. O'Leary
April 2005

Note to the Second Edition

This booklet was developed from three essays first published in 1953.[10] It contains the fruit of insight and experiences that filled the last years of Sigismund von Gleich's life.

He intended adding a further, concluding part, but his sudden death prevented him from doing so. Nevertheless, one can gain a sense of the direction which this would have taken. He would have accentuated the core content of his last text on *The Sources of Inspiration of Anthroposophy*,[11] which must be regarded as his spiritual legacy. He would have highlighted the soul-spiritual basis, the only possible stance and attitude of soul, for embarking on a transformation of the powers of evil.

To do so it is necessary to create that 'special moral atmosphere' which Rudolf Steiner says is the precondition for the perceptible activity of the Christ-impulse amongst human beings. In 1924 Rudolf Steiner suggested that a Christian spiritual community of autonomous individuals must arise from human souls' self-sacrificing will to work together and support one another. If we are to take the path of action that leads to the transformation of the powers of evil, the right atmosphere of moral etheric forces must first develop 'where the Christ Spirit can act in a quite new way which heals the conditions of human life. What is essential today is that a special, previously unknown spiritual willingness to sacrifice oneself for others awakens, one that is freely invoked and extends far beyond what we normally regard as moral conduct. Those who have awoken to the spirit have, after all, a duty to create compensation in the earth's etheric atmosphere for the immense powers of evil that have been unleashed.

Many years ago Rudolf Steiner appealed to his friends to acknowledge that 'anthroposophy consists of devoted self-sacrifice to what our times demand of us'.[12]

May the new impulses which Sigismund von Gleich imparted to human spiritual striving find their way to human hearts and fire our good will!

Magdalene von Gleich,
Zeist, Holland
27 September 1954

Note to the Third Edition

Ever more numerous are the voices raised to warn of outer and inner threats to humanity at the end of the twentieth century. To meet events consciously with a fundamentally positive and Christian attitude seems more necessary than ever. It was in this conviction that my father wrote these essays 30 years ago.

I have now added a Bibliography to the observations that form this new edition.

Dr Clemens-Christoph von Gleich
The Hague
February 1983

1. Sub-nature or Tartarus

Almost the last words that Rudolf Steiner—already lying fatally ill—wrote to members of the Anthroposophical Society shortly before his death[13] is the essay entitled 'From Nature to Sub-nature'. This was published as the nineteenth and last chapter of the book *The Michael Mystery*.[14]

Many friends[15] find it a deeply oppressive problem that their teacher departed from the earth shortly after writing such observations. This essay points with grave emphasis to realms of forces which seem ominous even to those who do not yet know that the adversary forces' field of activity, and thus the source of everything that inspires evil, is to be sought there.

Only today, now that we have some familiarity with the effects and impact of the sub-earthly realm of forces (as revealed in atom or hydrogen bombs), can we discern the truly prophetic warning in that article. Gaining even a half-way accurate idea of the devastating power of destruction of those forces—which have not only taken physical effect, but have also been activated in the spiritual realm of Inspiration since the advent of the 'atomic age'—can give us a sense of the serious responsibility we bear in the spiritual-scientific movement. Our future task must be to confront the solely earthly, mechanical forces that are now starting to be unleashed, and even the sub-earthly powers of a present and future 'super-technology', referred to in the statement that '...this is a world which emancipates itself from nature in a downwards direction'.[16]

We can also sense the spiritual obligation resting on us in

these words: 'Human beings must find the strength of an inner power of knowledge and perception to avoid being overwhelmed by Ahriman.'[17] We must still find what was not yet present when Rudolf Steiner died in 1925!

'Sub-nature must be understood for what it really is. This can only be done properly *if we rise in spiritual knowledge at least as far into extraterrestrial super-nature as we have descended, in the technical sciences, into sub-nature*.'[18]

As long ago as 1920, when technology leapt forward as a result of extensive use of electricity, enormous responsibilities were laid on mankind in the moral and intellectual sphere. These obligations increased exponentially 25 years later, when atomic technology reached the point of creating the first atomic explosions. Since then these sentences in Steiner's article have had a still truer and more insistent ring: 'Today very few people have an inkling of the important spiritual tasks which this implies for human beings. After its discovery, electricity was praised as the very soul of the natural world. Now, though, we must acknowledge its power to lead us downwards from nature to sub-nature!'[19]

These warnings have now become so urgent that we need to ask some earnest questions. Isn't it necessary, given the extraordinary onward march of technological inventions which have already led us into sub-earthly realms, to find— perhaps even before the end of the twentieth century—new ways in spiritual-scientific research that will enable serious seekers to keep spiritual pace with the almost unimaginable technological advances, by gaining insight into the forces of super-nature[20] with which we must connect ourselves? That final article which Steiner left us as legacy ends, after all, with words which can conjure up many questions: 'In a science of the spirit we now create another sphere which is wholly devoid of ahrimanic forces. By receiving knowledge of this spirituality, to which ahrimanic powers have no access, the human being is strengthened to oppose Ahriman *within the world*.'[21]

*

Reflecting on the composition of Steiner's innovative article we arrive at a threefold structure of all reality: *nature, super-nature and sub-nature*. Super-nature refers to the super-sensible spheres of the soul and spirit worlds, the realm of spirit in the cosmos. In nature itself we can distinguish two realms: first, that of physical laws, which have really coalesced out of the cosmos. These are, first and foremost, the sensory qualities and sensory-supersensible embodiments of colour, light, tone, etc. Here we are in the realm where nature itself is properly perceived.

In other words, we have not yet arrived at what is merely physical and earthly. That only starts with what is mechanical, with physical forces such as gravity, in which we are embedded while standing and walking. Thus, the purely physical, i.e. the mechanical, is integrated into semi-cosmic natural law. But here we are already at the border with sub-nature, just as sensory qualities take us to the boundary of cosmic super-nature.

The earthly is, therefore, a mediating field in which what is cosmically determined—from the realms of super-nature—encounters and penetrates the mechanical, which already belongs halfway to the sphere directly linked to the world which 'emancipates itself from nature in a downwards direction'.

We could only become free, self-aware ego-beings by living down into the 'purely earthly realm' and participating in the mechanical sciences as they have developed since Leonardo and Galileo. In the field of mechanics, therefore, we inevitably enter into a first contact with the sphere of sub-nature directly linked to it. There Ahriman, the adversary, holds sway. As Rudolf Steiner notes, the human being 'meets Ahriman as he lives his way in to what is solely earthly. With his own being he must now acquire the right relationship between his own being and the ahrimanic.'[22]

That is why, since the modern era began, science has inevitably and almost imperceptibly developed into technical knowledge and the handling of realms of forces that increasingly lead into the spheres of sub-nature, into the world 'which emancipates itself from nature in a downwards direction'. This is what has led to a situation where 'man lives to such an extent in a mechanical process of technical science that this has long imbued the scientific age with an entirely new quality'.[23]

Almost imperceptibly (since as long ago as the eighteenth century) we have slipped down from nature to sub-nature. On this path we first encountered the sphere of activity of electricity but mistakenly interpreted this as a supernatural element, i.e. as world soul (Schelling expressed this), although it belongs to sub-nature. The world of imperceptible electrical entities is one which Rudolf Steiner also characterized early on as a 'subsensible' realm.

What confusion and temptation was engendered in our human capacity for knowledge by the 'electricization' of nature during the course of the nineteenth century! Electricity pushed its way increasingly into the foreground in scientific explanations by philosopher-scientists, elbowing all other explanations out of the way. In trying to 'resolve' all visible nature into electrical entities, people were relieved of the effort involved in relating the sensory perceptions of natural phenomena to *ideas*. Instead, they believed they had discovered the primary 'thing in itself' in this form of the invisible. The human capacity for knowledge could be misled so easily here because electricity is the medium where the spirit of Ahriman manifests. Ahriman acts spiritually in human minds to deny the spirit, darkening the spiritual ether light of ideas!

Thus, this earthly, physical nature, and within it the human being, forms a 'centre' between the two opposing force realms of super-nature (the cosmic and spiritual) and sub-nature (the subsensible or sub-earthly). Physical nature is affected and penetrated by both spheres: the qualitative and sensory from 'above' and the quantitative, mechanical from 'below'.

If we wish to preserve our endangered humanity which, in the recent past and in the dawning future, is at risk of falling prey to the mechanistic, sub-natural realm of super-technology—as can also be witnessed, very alarmingly, in our fall into subhuman modes of behaviour—we will increasingly have to see our task as ascending at least as far into the supersensible spheres of super-nature in spiritual perception and moral and spiritual practice as, due to technological practices, we have involuntarily plunged our will into the power realms of ahrimanic sub-nature. In Steiner's words: 'Our age needs knowledge that rises above nature because it must deal inwardly with a dangerous life content that has sunk below nature.'[24]

Thus, we initially need to become ever better acquainted with the particular characteristics and laws at work in the dangerous ahrimanic realm of sub-nature so as to see, subsequently, from which supersensible realms of divine super-nature we can draw the corresponding counter-forces. Only then can we think of seeking the higher spheres and impulses from such spheres, with which we must unite, in order to find the inner powers of perception and the strength of spirit that enable us 'to avoid being overwhelmed by Ahriman in technical culture'.

It is likely that this will involve the all-embracing action of forces that work destructively from below and healingly from above, in whose mutual interplay people of coming centuries will find themselves embedded. In order to be able to meet the great and perhaps wholly unexpected challenges of our era, we will have to acquaint ourselves with both streams of forces to prevent ourselves from slipping blindly and ever further into ahrimanic sub-nature—a process which, disturbingly enough, has already begun. And we will need to learn to draw on the spiritual sources of the higher worlds in order to acquire that strength of spirit (will this not be almost magical in the future?) which enables us to banish the highly dangerous forces from below or, better still, to transform them into benevolent, healing impulses.

*

We owe many hints and images of the sub-earthly world to the fading wisdom of ancient Greece. We may first recall Hades, the 'underworld', and then in a broader sense the whole realm of the 'enemies of the gods', the Titans, who were cast down into Tartarus. *Phaidon*, Plato's still little-understood dialogue about immortality and the sphere of the dead, grants us insight into the sub-earthly realm. It is hard to decide, though, to what extent the images contained in it relate to physical sub-earthly realities or supersensible ones. In most cases we will be correct in thinking of them as sensory-supersensible realities that best correspond to ancient Greek perceptions.

Of the various underworld rivers, some flow around the earth. But most of them flow below its surface through many caverns and subterranean channels. Plato chiefly names the following: Acheron, Periphlegeton, Styx and Kokytos. All of the subterranean chasms, it is said, are linked to one another through other, narrower channels, bearing the waters of each to the others, and sometimes also flowing into a lake. It is stated that 'there are inexhaustible rivers of incalculable size below the earth, of springs both hot and cold and a great fire, mighty rivers of fire; and also streams of liquid mud, in some cases pure and clean, and in other cases dirty and fouled'.[25]

The largest of the chasms, plunging right through the whole earth, is named 'the Abyss' by Homer, and Tartarus by other poets. All rivers flow together into Tartarus and also flow out again. Acheron flows under the earth through wide waste areas. Periphlegeton, in contrast, pours into a broad area of mighty fire not far from its source, where it forms a giant lake bigger than our (Mediterranean) sea, boiling with water and mud. After various subterranean detours, it then pours at its very deepest point into Tartarus. From this fire river, Periphlegeton, small bubbles are spewed out in volcanoes. In a contrary direction to this river, the Styx flows into a lake in a wild, eerie, dark blue region. This river of death also plunges into the depths of the earth, winds around and emerges again opposite Periphlegeton. The fourth river is the Kokytos.

Everywhere in this region the souls of the dead must do penance for their misconduct until they have been purified.

The Styx is described in one place as follows: 'The waterfalls of the Styx do not just vanish forever; but they are lost eternally to all motions of life. They are the image of death that is capable of no reawakening.'

We will encounter this death sphere again in the spiritual-scientific description of the sub-earthly domain.

We must imagine Tartarus itself in deeper subterranean vaults. The temple wisdom of the ancients hinted at some of its secrets in pictorial and mythological descriptions. We can chiefly think of Hesiod's *Theogony* here, which does not just systematically describe the realm of the upper gods, but also the underworld realm of the inhabitants of Tartarus. Hades, the sphere of the chthonic gods, passes over into the sub-earthly realm of the adversary gods. The significance of the names and images connected with these beings can reveal much to us of the spiritual forces at work in sub-nature.

Eternal, intrinsic and personified darkness (Erebus) holds sway in the gloomy realms of underworld Tartarus. At its entrance stands the palace of Original Night (Nyx). Let us turn here to a description by Hesiod:

Before all else arose Chaos, but straight away there came
Gaia, broad-breasted, becoming for all an eternal domain.
Those who dwell up on Olympus's snowy peaks: the gods;
Tartarus, ghastly and gloomy: in the womb of the spacious earth ...
Erebus then and dark Nyx sprang up and arose from the chaos.
From Nyx came forth as further scion Hemera and Aether,
To whom she gave birth after joining in loving embrace with Erebus ...
Again she gave birth, to the Cyclops, offspring wild and defiant:
Brontes, Steropes too and Arges, audacious in spirit,
Who handed the thunder to Zeus, who forged the lightning flashes.
In appearance they wholly resembled the higher gods immortal,
Except for the single eye positioned centrally in their forehead.

That was the cause of the name that was given to each, of
   Cyclops:
The round eye placed there centrally in the midst of their
   forehead;
The work though testified to strength, to power and
   invention.
Three other sons too Gaia, in loving embrace with Uranus,
Gave birth to: mighty in strength, whose names must not
   be spoken!
Kottos, Briareos then, and Gyes of evil pride.
From each one's shoulder sprang a hundred gigantic arms,
Ugly in shape; and fifty horrendous heads held sway,
Ruling from each shoulder a thick-set assembly of limbs,
Unequalled force indwelling the mighty body of each.
For, of all the offspring which Gaia gave Father Uranus,
These were the most ghastly, even Uranus abhorred them.
No sooner born than he hid them deep in the earth, and
   kept them
Far from the light of day: rejoiced at his dark crime even.
Yet the burdened Earth sighed deep and groaning planned
   revenge.

We should note that the sub-earthly beings are expressly
stated to be descended from the upper gods, who are amal-
gamated in 'Uranus'. This points to a mysterious link
between the subterranean powers and supersensible, divine
beings.

Without intellectually dissipating the resonant imagery of
these mythical visions, one can still try to gain certain concepts from their primal realities. What we nowadays think of
as the threefold world of super-nature, nature (the physical
realm) and sub-nature was referred to in Greek mythology as
Uranus, Gaia and Tartarus.

Without addressing the third realm, that of Tartarus, Rudolf Steiner once said that the Mystery School vision of Uranus and Gaia should not primarily be viewed as ascribing male and female qualities to these two figures, nor 'as if the one was of absolute value and the other absolutely worthless. They were conceived as a polarity that exists within a unity, as though these were two opposite poles of a single thing. Uranus represents the peripheral, encircling realm whose polar opposite is the point at the centre, Gaia.'[26]

Rudolf Steiner was pointing here to the polarity of the cosmos's centrifugal 'universal' forces and the centripetal 'core' forces, which also come to expression in the human being's physiological and psychological polarities.[27]

At the end of Goethe's time there were still researchers who could lovingly immerse themselves in the spiritual pictures contained in mythology, and gain insight into something of their wisdom. I am thinking here of Emil Braun (1809–56), who provided an instructive survey of the realms of Olympus and Tartarus in his *Griechische Götterlehre*.

In accordance with Hesiod's *Theogony* he compiled the beings in Tartarus, the 'bowels' of the earth, as a threefold unity, thus arriving at a ninefold division of the under-world:

a) The Cyclops

(i) Brontes (ii) Steropes (iii) Arges

Their names clearly reveal all elements of inflammable electrical power, without separating out what appears there as a single entity through arbitrary, analytic distinctions. Brontes embodies the roll of thunder which cannot be separated from the discharge of an electric spark. Steropes is the celestially bright illumination of lightning. And Arges is the silver-shimmering element of primal fire, which is as little able to enter this phenomenological world as is primal light.

b) The wives of the Cyclops

(iv) Ischys   (v) Bia   (vi) Mechane

The ancients gave pictorial expression to these malleable forces in the image of domestic femininity. The wives of the Cyclops are clearly named *support, strength* and *creative drive*. If one thinks of them engaged in smithying, Ischys holds the tongs, Bia delivers the hammer strokes and Mechane is active between them, in a malleable, purposeful way.

c) The Hekatoncheires (hundred-armed beings)

(vii) Kottos   (viii) Briareus   (ix) Gyes

Multi-headedness is not meant but, on the contrary, in this triad the unity of the will is particularly accentuated. Kottos is an outmoded dialectical term that only appears in sub-forms and conflated words, but invariably means 'head'. Once one has arrived at this concept one needs only short reflection to resolve a *group* of people or animals into innumerable numbers of individuals, each furnished with a head. The concept of multiplicity comes to the fore much more strongly still in the diverse use of the limbs which Gyes embodies, while Briareus is more an embodiment of the might of the body in relation to its mass, which the species represents in its entirety, or the unity of substance out of which the life of each individual emerges (page 56).

Such conceptual deductions and primal meanings ulti-mately lead, no doubt, to useful ideas of the properties of the subterranean Tartarus powers. The time will eventually come when we are able to fully acknowledge these initial attempts at interpretation using spiritual-scientific descriptions of ahrimanic laws and forces.

But, before we can pass on to such descriptions, we should briefly mention the characterization of sub-nature which we owe to the Pythagorean Mystery School. I am referring here to the difficult idea of 'counter-earth' (anti-Chthon). This is sometimes ascribed to Pythagoras's pupil Hiketas, and has come down to us as follows. Between the earth and the planetary spheres surrounding it on the one hand, and on the other the central fire of the universe—the divine hearth Hestia radiating light and heat—lies the 'counter-earth'. It is due to this that Hestia is hidden from human eyes. Since a spatial and concentric interpretation of this barely makes sense, the question arises whether it may indicate a more occult idea: the inner-tellurian Tartarus of ahrimanic powers works upwards into the surface realm of earth in such a way that the pure, virginal, holy primal light of the universe—the central life-fire of all things (to use Böhme's term) which is connected with the working of spiritual sun forces—is hidden from human perception through the obscuring force of anti-Chthon.

We must hold fast here to the basic vision of the threefold world with which we began. Earthly humanity dwelling amidst earthly nature is subject to the dual influences from above and from below. Both are partly determined by the forces of super-nature and sub-nature.

Since we human beings are also partly influenced by the obscuring forces from below, we interpret many things on earth that actually emanate from above in terms of the lower world of forces. For example, we may regard the heavenly astral light and colour qualities as mere vibrations of a colourless 'something'.

And starting from ancient times, alongside all phenomen-ological interpretations we have of course developed all kinds of *atomistic* explanations of nature which more or less de-soul the earth. This has been further reinforced by electrodynamic explanations of matter. Ultimately we have even de-spiritualized the world of the heavens through *celestial mechanics*.

In the pure observation of the glory of nature's colours we can still receive the reflection of the cosmos within the earthly realm! But we are partly influenced by the counter-earth. This influence even gains the upper hand in the most recent scientific theories and hypotheses. The only way in which we can find the right stance towards the whole of reality is by having the courage to acknowledge that the soul-spiritual forces of the cosmos (super-nature) work together with sub-sensible forces on our earth, such as sub-nature's electro-magnetic forces. The forces of Uranus participate in Gaia, but so too do those of Tartarus!

2. The Layers of the Interior of the Earth

The introductory essay on sub-nature or Tartarus (the Abyss) tried to show that nature, or the earthly realm, is partly affected by super-nature and partly by sub-nature. The beings of Tartarus, as offspring of Uranus and Gaia, are half-earthly and half-divine in origin it is true, but they became counter-forces to the heavenly spheres. One could say that they are perverted, 'abhorred' divine forces that were, therefore, cast down into the underworld.

Nevertheless, they remain related in nature to divine beings. They have the same qualities, but these assume reversed, opposite conditions. That is why, in their entirety, they not only form the counter-earth, but also (if one may call the entirety of the divine spheres the *Logos*) one can see them as the contrasting, sub-earthly sphere of the *Anti-Logos*. Dante calls the leader of this sphere Lucifer, who dwells in the city of Dis within the earth's interior. This must be a quite different being from the one generally referred to as Lucifer in spiritual-scientific literature.

The underworld beings have opposite forces and qualities to all those in the super-earthly sphere. In them lies the source of all *destruction and annihilation*. It is for this very reason that Goethe has the corrupting spirit Mephistopheles, whom he names the 'strange son of chaos', oppose the divine armies as leader of all adversary forces. Interestingly, he puts these words into his mouth:

I am the spirit that always will negate.
And rightly so, for all things that arise
Fully deserve their own demise.

Far better if nothing ever came to life:
For all that you call sin, call strife
Destruction, evil, in a word, is where
My element is, the sphere that I prefer.

Is he right to assert 'And rightly so'? That the 'strange son of chaos' does not lie when he calls himself 'part of that power which would evil constantly do, and constantly does the good' is confirmed by God in the Prologue of *Faust*, who ascribes *positive* functions to Mephistopheles in the cosmos:

Man all too easily grows slack
And rest is soon his only wish;
Therefore I'm glad your devilish
Influence spurs him on to act.

The spirit of negation, of opposition, obstacles and resistance is essential in the whole plan of creation. The spheres of the Anti-Logos are also called upon to play a co-creating role.

Many parts of *Faust* testify to the fact that Goethe was deeply initiated into the mysteries of *evil*, which are also those of the interior of the earth. One only has to look at the scenes in Auerbach's cellar, in the Witch's Kitchen and in the northern Walpurgis Night, which come close to characterizing black magic practices. Rudolf Steiner referred to this in the seventh lecture on 'Initiate Consciousness', a series that was advertised in Torquay in the summer of 1924 under the title 'True and False Paths in Spiritual Investigation'. Here Steiner strongly emphasizes the powerful dangers of these spheres and mysteries of evil, a theme on which he clearly focused very intensely at the end of his life. Why this was the case becomes apparent in the same lecture, which speaks of the particular needs of human evolution in the Michael Age.

If one imagines Steiner's spiritual activity continuing in

close connection with those evolutionary necessities after his death, then one can perhaps suggest that today he would, among other things, begin to speak about the forces of the earth's interior, about the devastating powers of evil which increasingly threaten mankind with destruction. At the same time he would also speak about the spiritual-scientific means which the new Christ-impulse of the second half of the twentieth century offers to counter these appalling dangers.

For this reason it seems high time to penetrate with new insights what Rudolf Steiner said between 1906 and 1909 about the soul-spiritual structure of the interior of the earth.

Goethe already knew that the powers of evil, or of negation, have been locked in the earth's interior since ancient times, and that they spew forth every now and then in volcanic eruptions. He has Mephistopheles relate this truth as an eyewitness in the fourth act of *Faust* Part II, giving to the initially enlightened and scientifically sceptical Faust this quiet aside:

> How devils observe nature I must say,
> Is actually very interesting to see.

In the 'high mountains' where they arrived, Mephistopheles noted that the place had once been the depths of hell. Since Faust chuckles about such an 'idiotic legend', Mephistopheles elaborates very earnestly:

> When God the Lord—I still remember why—
> Banished us from the air to deepest drop,
> Where glowing at the core eternal fire
> Burned its way through the abyss without stop,
> We found ourselves in too much brightness lit,
> In very cramped, uncomfortable condition.
> The devils all were seized with a coughing fit,
> They spat and spewed all round without remission;

Hell swelled with sulphur stink and sourness
What fumy gas! Becoming so extreme
That soon, despite its thickness, surface crust
Of earth above exploded, spurting steam.
So now this all has shifted and the ground
Before of hell is raised up into summit.
This may also teach you how to found
The doctrine of reversing what is deepest
Into what is highest; for we fled
From servile hot abyss into excess
Mastery of open air instead.
An open secret, well preserved and sealed
That will be long before it is revealed. (Eph. 6:12)

*

I was present when, bubbling up beneath,
The abyss swelled and streaming fire bore;
When Moloch's hammer welding cliff to cliff
Mountain rubble flung and scattered far...
The land still groans with alien bulk and mass:
Who can explain what power scattered thus?

Finally, however, Mephistopheles also refers to the moral aspect, hinting at the huge spiritual power of the subterranean forces:

A matter of honour—the devil was involved.
Our folk's achievements are both great and fine.
Tumult, power, confusion! See the sign!

To the description that the devils were hurled into the 'excess mastery of open air' through volcanic forces, Goethe adds a reference to Paul's Epistle to the Ephesians, where, in Chapter 6, we read:

> Put on the whole armour of God, that ye may be able to stand against the wiles of the devil. For we wrestle not against flesh and blood, but against the Principalities, against the Powers, against the rulers of darkness of this world, against spiritual wickedness in high places.[28]

The fact that these adversarial powers and this 'prince of darkness' (Ahriman) do not just hold sway in the darkness of the Abyss, but also in the wider atmosphere, was something Goethe found expressed in Chapter 2 of the same letter by Paul.[29] Texts well known to him, by certain Rosicrucian masters such as Georg von Welling, describe these super-sensible facts in more detail, referring to the ghost spheres of the atmosphere.

Hints found in such Christian texts confirm the picture presented above that the counter-earth forces are also definitely active above the ground. Thus, thanks to ahrimanic obscuring of the capacity for knowledge, the central spiritual fire of things is rendered invisible. The projection of certain Tartarean powers into the upper air, as it were, intervenes between the seven planetary spheres and their lowest body, the moon, on the one hand, and the earth on the other. There, in the 'province of air', as it were in an 'eighth sphere', is the ruling throne of Ahriman, in 'excess mastery of open air'. He is banished there, however, and kept at a distance from earthly humanity through the benevolent moon wisdom of Jehovah.

It is a very profound insight of Goethe that the ahrimanic 'prince of the air' is a '*part* of that power which would do evil constantly'. The other part is, in fact, not to be sought 'in the north-western province of air' but, in the depths of the earth's interior, as the all-consuming Moloch.

It is also worth recalling how Faust becomes aware of Mephistopheles in the first place. Faust, as it were, summons

the presence of ahrimanic air spirits when, in luciferic ego-
tism, overweening pride and earth-outstripping knowledge,
he calls out during the Easter walk:

O there are spirits in the air
Weaving between the earth and sky:
Descend from your golden mists to me,
Bear me to new life bright and fair!
Give me a magic coat to carry me off
To distant lands, O bear me far away.

This is a reference to Mephistopheles' magic cloak, which he
uses for his travels with Faust after first preparing a 'little fire-
air'.

Wagner immediately senses how dangerous it might be to
summon these tempters, becomes anxious and, in consequence, draws the ahrimanic powers still more forcefully
towards them:

Do not summon this too familiar throng,
Who spread abroad within the mists of air,
Thousandfold dangers do they bring,
From every corner hurrying here.

Then, perhaps in reference to the profound hints regarding
the working of the powers of evil found in Chapter 7 of the
Book of Daniel, he characterizes the elemental forces
underlying the spiritual forces of evil, which in enmity come
storming towards human beings from the four directions of
the compass. And there, already, comes Mephistopheles,
circling out of the distance in the shape of a poodle...

*

At this point let us turn to a spiritual-scientific description of
subterranean forces of evil. Rudolf Steiner was the first to

speak of them (in response to dreadful volcanic eruptions and earthquakes in 1906 and 1908), mainly at the end of his lecture cycle *At the Gates of Spiritual Science*[30] given in Stuttgart in the summer of 1906, but also before that on 21 April 1906,[31] and once again on 12 June of the same year in Paris. Edouard Schuré commented on Rudolf Steiner's 18 Paris lectures in the Foreword to this lecture cycle, published in English as *An Esoteric Cosmology*.[32] In addition, on 1 January 1909 in Berlin, in response to the appalling earthquake at Messina, Steiner gave a lecture on 'Mephistopheles and Earthquakes'.[33] He probably also referred to these phenomena elsewhere.

A study by one of his pupils is also relevant here: the lecture by Adolf Arenson on 22 January 1914 entitled *The Interior of the Earth*.[34] This study, in which Arenson gives a major key to the subject, undoubtedly met with Rudolf Steiner's approval. We thus leave the realm of mythological or poetic imagery and veiled suggestion, and now meet a spiritual-scientific description of sub-nature in a form appropriate to our time—though one that still needs further elaboration in future.

Goethe's pupil Carl Gustav Carus believed that the earth was not a sphere of solid mass but a hollow sphere, just as all organic life begins with the primal form of an egg cell. The earth, too, he said, is a living being, and the thickness of its crust amounts to only a ninth of the radius of the earth (around 700 km[35]). Towards its interior, the crust quickly heats up and, at a depth of about 22 to 25 miles (35–40 km), it 'passes over into the condition of a melting furnace', and then, in the earth's hollow interior, 'all that is reasonably possible to imagine is the etheric and nebulous primal matter of which the earth was first formed'.[36]

This is then augmented by the following further conjecture:

In general one can, therefore, state with some certainty that the four or five hundred volcanoes on the earth, of which only a smaller proportion are currently active, are the tellurian oceans by means of which the earth's interior—i.e. the abyss of flowing lava fire underneath the whole earth's surface—continually remains in connection with this surface and the atmosphere itself.

This view of the earth-shell is confirmed by spiritual research, although it depicts the hollow interior of the earth as less benign:

> The occult sciences of all epochs have stated the following about the interior of the earth. We must think of the earth as consisting of a series of layers, not completely separated from one another like the skins of an onion, but which merge into one another gradually. The uppermost layer, the mineral mass, is related to the interior as an eggshell is to an egg. This topmost layer is called the mineral earth.[37]

Physical observations tell us only about the very outermost, relatively thin and also delicate shell of the earth, whose permeability is demonstrated by volcanic eruptions. Boring tools take us no further down than two thousand metres or so. Most researchers assume that the solid crust of the earth is between 40 and 120 kilometres in thickness, the lower layers of which are, however, perhaps already malleable and viscous. One finds other conclusions by authors such as A. Ritter and S. Günther,[38] who imagine the inner strata as being fluid and gaseous. Due to the enormous temperatures in the depths, they believe that even the greatest pressure levels could not render these gases fluid. Günther imagines seven zones: first, solid crust; second, latent plasticity; third, viscous fluid such as magma; fourth, normal fluid; fifth, normal gas; sixth, gas in a 'critical' condition; seventh, the core of the earth composed of homogeneous gases. This concept is the closest to spiritual-scientific descriptions, which state the following.

If we were to penetrate into the interior of the earth, below its mineral crust, the deeper we went, the more confusing we would find conditions there. What we would encounter is so dissimilar to processes on the earth's surface that we really do not have words to describe it. While still in the mineral stratum we would encounter silver in as fluid a state as quicksilver (mercury), and the other metals likewise. At a considerable depth we would then find cavernous hollows that extend downwards in channels into still deeper layers. Under certain circumstances particular substances are forced upwards with great impetus through these channels—for example, during volcanic eruptions.

Before we go on to describe still deeper layers, we first need to sketch some fundamental aspects about their connection with past stages of Earth evolution.

During the course of aeons the earth has not only grown more solid and mineralized through a contracting and densifying process, but has also significantly diminished in size due to all kinds of expelling processes. Originally the earth extended very far in the form of extremely fine substance, in fact encompassing everything that now makes up the whole planetary system. At that time there was only a single, etherically very fine and tenuous planetary body in the planetary system. Uranus, the totality of the planetary heavens, and Gaia, the earth being, were then still merged as one, deeply penetrating and fertilizing one another.

If we wish to characterize the separation of this unified totality precisely, however, we have to say that, in separating out and differentiating itself, this original single whole split into the heavenly world above, while in a downwards direction the primal divine nature of the earth was partly transformed into the counter-divine yet held together by the solidity of earth. By so doing, though, this latter portion came under the dual influence of super-nature and sub-nature. The spheres of the counter-divine are the essence of negative, adversarial forces in conflict with all divine, creative potencies. One could say that as the differentiated external planetary system emerged out of the overall cosmic body, first giving rise to the sun spirit and later the moon soul, something like a lower sediment was deposited in the depths of the earth which became the spheres and forces of the earth's interior.

This process corresponds to a general evolutionary rule which also cited:

> When one force begins to work in the universe another force opposed to the first arises at the same moment. Everything that happens in the world is subject to the law of polarity. Thus, to the degree that the free activity of the divine, the light, the creative and the good arise, at the same time there must also arise their counter-pole and sediment: the sub-earthly (hell), darkness, destruction and evil.[39]

Therefore, every heavenly sphere and power of the divine hierarchies has a corresponding sub-earthly sphere of counter-hierarchies. Analogous to this, all creative forces and substances or nature principles (such as physical, etheric and astral, etc.) have their counterpart in contrary, destructive sub-natural principles in the earth's interior. Despite this, all sub-earthly counter-hierarchies were originally nothing other than the *brothers*, left behind, of beings who ascended upwards. And the fact that they remain in the earth's depths was initially a sacrifice on their part.

The *human being*, who remains at the *centre of existence*, has the task in the second half of world evolution to redeem the sub-earthly forces, in spiritual fraternity with the Divine Mediator and the upper powers.

The sub-earthly counter-realms of the deeper layers of earth only gradually arose or became active as spheres of anti-divine negation, opposition and obstruction in the course of successive cosmic separations from the cosmic body's original primal totality. Thus, we can understand descriptions in spiritual science that the three uppermost layers of the earth's interior only formed after the moon separated from the earth, and the three middle layers formed in consequence of the sun's departure from the earth. Now, alongside certain physically hardened substances, other etheric and astral forces are connected with the moon, while the actual worlds of spirit are connected with the sun. At the very primal beginnings, when Saturn formed out of the cosmic body, the innermost three layers of the interior of the earth formed, where 'primal evil' is centred.

Accordingly, in the three uppermost layers of the earth one finds the counter-forces to all forces of physical structure and development, of etheric life and of astrality or soul. Further down we find the spiritual counter-forces to those creative archetypal realms of the spirit-land which, as divine thoughts, constitute the spiritual principles of nature and human beings as described in Rudolf Steiner's book *Theosophy*.

Whereas the noble and divine aim of all upper powers is the human being in his divine fulfilment and perfection, the sub-earthly powers, in contrast, aim to create a negative sevenfold or ninefold counter-entity to the human being, and thus, also, the real antichrist, who is at the same time the Anti-humanus.

Paul spoke of this entity and his preparation by the 'mysteries of evil' in Chapter Two of the Second Epistle to the

Thessalonians. It is a shocking apocalypse.[40] How this power will affect humanity is described in the third chapter of the Second Epistle to Timothy.[41]

The activity of these mysteries of evil has now become clearly discernible in our times. But for that very reason, too, the new, benevolent spirit forces of Christ and humanity have come into effect.

That is why it is high time to examine how the increasingly dangerous forces of the earth's interior can be transformed through corresponding spiritual impulses.

If we now cast a broad look over the nine spheres of the sub-earthly realm, we can briefly summarize the various descriptions by Rudolf Steiner that are available to us.

1. The solid or mineral earth. This contains all mineral substances. The physical is not the same as the mineral. As such the physical is invisible and non-material. It is composed of will substance and mechanical laws. Only where the physical is filled with mineral substance do we have matter, which becomes finer in state as we proceed downwards. Below the mineral earth, however, is something which cannot be compared with any form of substance:

2. The life layer: the fluid or soft earth. One can sometimes observe residues and signs of this semi-fluid layer in a calm ocean, when small islets suddenly appear and then vanish again. Due to the departure of the moon from the earth, no doubt a considerable part of the mineral layer is missing from the ocean floor there, and can now be seen instead on the moon's surface.

This layer has very special properties, for it is here that substance begins to have spiritual characteristics. One can say that it has dull, plantlike sensation. But if one brought it into connection with something living, the latter's life would immediately be driven out of it and destroyed. Due to this life-extinguishing power, one can speak of a real death sphere, of the Styx. The expansion force of this layer is so great that, without the restraining pressure of the mineral layer, it would scatter on all sides into the cosmos.

3. The air earth is also called *vapour earth, steam earth* or the *awareness stratum.* This is the counter-pole to soul astrality, which also departed from the earth with the moon. As steam seeks to escape from a kettle, so too does the steam layer seek to escape from the earth. It is a substance which destroys sensation and feeling, transforming all feeling qualities (such as enjoyment or pain) into their opposite.

4. The soul earth, also called the *form earth* or *water earth.* This layer consists of a substance that makes a material counterpart of everything that happens in the spirit realm. Here we have the negative counter-images to physical things. The form is, as it were, transformed into its opposite. All properties move into the surrounding space, while the space itself that the object occupied is empty.

5. The fruit earth (growth earth or seed earth) is bursting with exuberant energy. Each particle of it immediately grows like fungus, becomes ever larger and can only be kept in by the upper layers. If a part of the fruit earth could reach the upper air, forms would continually grow from it and vanish again. This layer, as it were, possesses soul. In it a tendency to enormous expansion holds sway, dispersal into cosmic space.

6. The fire earth (or passion earth)[42] is a highly sensitive zone, the source of immeasurably extreme, unharnessed feelings and passions. Thus, it reacts very strongly to human excesses of will and outbreaks of passion. If one were to exert pressure on this reservoir of will forces, it would defend itself and respond with impulsive resistance. This zone can burst via channels through all the zones above it and have appallingly devastating effects in earthquakes and volcanic eruptions. The primal fire forces are banished to this realm, which is the material kingdom of Ahriman-Mephistopheles. Ahriman is chained in the earth's interior while his other 'part' in the 'air province' of the eighth sphere, between the earth and the moon, is closely linked in terms of its forces with the fire earth.

7. *The mirror layer* of the earth, also called the *earth mirror* (the *reflector earth* or *earth reverser*).[43] Everything that happens on the earth's surface manifests here in a negative, reversed form. If one beats on metal on the earth's surface, in the mirror layer it would emit a tone by itself. The 'mirror' resembles a prism that splits all things, reflects them and allows them to appear in complementary properties. All spirit in nature is here transformed into its corresponding opposite, so that, for example, light becomes electricity. Arenson states: 'Its substance transforms everything into its opposite. Everything that one can imagine as moral qualities in human nature is here turned into its opposite.'[44]

In this seventh layer one meets the counter-principle to the divine, human ego-being, which originates in the fourth region of spirit-land, while in the next layer we encounter the counter-forces to the fifth region of spirit-land.

8. *The fragmenter, slicer or dismemberer* (also called the s*plintering earth* or e*xplosive earth*).[45] Named the *number creator* by the School of Pythagoras because it endlessly multiplies all single entities. It also fragments everything of a moral nature. Through the energy it exerts on earth, this layer is to blame for division, unhappiness, dispute, disharmony and hatred. Dante described this zone as Caina or Cain's ravine in the depths of hell's crater.[46] This layer brought the substance of evil into the world. Humanity's development of love and fraternity involves a continual overcoming of this layer. We will return to this later.

9. *The earth core.* This conceals two great secrets. On the

one hand it is the domain of the planetary spirit and has three organs, two of which can be compared with our brain and heart. On the other hand it is from here that the power of spiritual evil emanates, and thus what also gives rise to black magic.

In Dante's poem we find the city of Dis in the ninth circle of hell, where Lucifer is seen in the icy abyss with a threefold countenance that is coloured red, yellow and black, perhaps indicating the primal vices of anger, avarice and laziness.

I will describe further characteristics of the nine layers of earth in the third part of this study, where the focus will be mainly on the new Christ forces of strength and goodness, through which the human being will in future be able to transform evil forces into good.[47]

3. May the Power of Goodness Transform All Evil

Christ is the mediator between heaven and earth. He reconciles the human being with God and also—through the forces of super-nature—saves all creatures from the destructive forces of sub-nature. He acquired all these capacities through the deed of sacrifice at Golgotha, and will achieve this with the help of those who wish to follow him wherever he leads.

Since the Middle Ages, the sevenfold path of Christ's passion, as described by St John, has become a focus of meditation for mystical and religious souls, and at times also a Christian path of initiation. Such a profoundly soulful 'discipleship of Christ' led pupils through severe self-denial to an inner spiritual experience of the Foot-washing, Scourging, Crowning with Thorns, Cross-bearing, Mystic Death, Burial and Resurrection.

Today, too, this path of the soul, alongside the newer Rosicrucian one, is certainly fruitful. Only on *this* path, which closely follows Christ as the one who overcame death, can the secrets of the earth's interior be investigated. Rudolf Steiner expressly emphasized this. But beyond this, these experiences also help in the healing transformation of hell's powers of evil.

On earth Christ gave the nine Beatitudes, which showed even the simplest people how they can work towards such a goal through moral self-transformation. But what was decisive for this was not a doctrine, but a deed of sacrifice. Christ overcame the destructive forces of the earth's interior through his path of suffering and his subsequent Descent into Hell. Ascending to the heavens soon after the Resurrection, he implanted his death-defeating forces into all celestial spheres, so that certain spiritual impulses could make it possible for human beings of later times to master all sub-earthly powers of evil. These divine forces were, therefore, intended to benefit the earth as soon as—thanks to the new Christ era—the threshold to the spiritual world was opened. Thus also are opened the 'nine paths' which spiritual science will eventually be able to reveal for the overcoming of evil. Today we can only have a faint inkling of these things.

The Descent into Hell between the Crucifixion and Resurrection was one of Christ's most significant redeeming deeds. The spiritual researcher Rudolf Steiner testified to this in one of the lectures illuminating the secrets of the earth's interior:

> It is more than just a figure of speech to say that, at the moment that his death occurred on Golgotha, Christ appeared in the realm of the shades and, in a certain sense, cast Ahriman into chains. This is definite *occult fact*, even if Ahriman's influence remains, and is responsible for all materialistic ideas. He can be paralysed when people try to understand the event of Golgotha, and draw from this the strength to return to the spiritual world.[48]

Sooner or later the spiritual scientist will find in higher realms those spirit impulses of Christ which have become active there as a fruit of his Descent into Hell and Ascension.

There have always been exceptional destinies that enabled some people to experience Christ's path of suffering in physical and soul form—leading even to the stigmata—above all during Passiontide. Such souls were blessed with a clairvoyant vision of Christ's passion. One very notable proclaimer of the Christ Mystery was the pious Katharina Emmerich from Dülmen (1745–1824). Clemens Brentano published her moving reports of this. In describing her vision of the Descent into Hell she related the following remarkable vision:

> In the centre was an abyss of darkness. Lucifer was cast into it, in chains, and thick black vapours seethed around him ... I heard that Lucifer, if I am not mistaken, would be freed again for a while some 50 or 60 years before AD 2000. I have forgotten many other dates that I heard.[49]

This suggests a date of 1940/50. Do not the confusion and turbulence in civilization since then show that the terrible forces of sub-nature have been unchained? The gates of hell *have indeed opened.* So we can understand why Rudolf Steiner before his death referred so earnestly to the dangers of sub-nature.[50]

The uprush of the forces from the abyss is already in motion. The counter-realm of sub-nature is already active amongst us!

But for the past 40 or so years[51] we have also known that the new power of Christ shall, at the same time, also become active from the world of etheric life as a powerful aid.

This time has arrived! The new Christ era has already begun!

At the Ascension, Christ became the Lord on earth of all heavenly forces. Since then these heavenly forces have contained all sources of strength or spiritual impulses for strengthening those who wish to achieve increasing mastery of the sub-earthly forces of evil. The time has come when powerful forces of good descend from above to help in the terribly hard-fought battle of spirits.

In relation to the possible transformation of the evil of sub-nature through these powerful forces of good from super-nature, I would like to survey the two corresponding force realms once more. For various reasons, however, this can only be sketched in outline.

I

The solid earth was originally built up according to its material and physical structure and geological distinctions. But it will be 'unbuilt' or dissolved again in the second half of earth evolution in which we are already now living—and perhaps more quickly than we suspect. Spontaneous radio-active decay of certain substances seems to indicate this. For this reason there may be devastating earth movements in coming centuries. Ultimately all four elements will have to pass over into quite different states of existence. It is only since the end of the Atlantean epoch that they have their current structure.

That the earth must be pulverized and disintegrate lies in the karmic law of the earth's genesis. But such disintegration through anti-physical powers can occur in a variety of ways. Geological and climatological transformations must come and will not be without severe catastrophes. However, the same divine power which, through 'Genesis', once became Lord of the earth[52] will in the future—and united with Christ—work in such a way that, despite all alterations to the earth's surface, a new basis will be there for human beings upon which they can fulfil their God-willed evolutionary tasks. For these purposes there will, no doubt, be occasions for more severe, but also for benevolent and rightful, edu-cational 'interventions' by the divine powers.

In times when the earth disintegrates, the *inner Jehovah impulse* will indeed become active. This will allow karmically necessary earthquake catastrophes to occur in accordance with Christ's intentions, so that we can once more learn to trust in the words of David's Psalm: 'Blessed be he whom thou, O Jehovah, punisheth and teacheth through thy law.'

II

In our times we can receive the new Christ help from the etheric realms of life. We cannot yet tell in what diverse ways the re-enlivening of human etheric forces will in future work against life-destroying influences from the soft earth (the second telluric layer), since this will also partly depend on human beings. Various contemporary phenomena are showing us how disturbingly their influences are increasing: the cynical lack of sacredness and humanity in everything connected with reproduction; the lack of a common awareness of community and shared experience of human suffering; and the powerlessness to discern and perceive things with insight. All this points to an increasing weakening of the etheric forces.

Who is unaware of the unavoidable necessity to counter the biological degeneration passed on from one generation to the next? External means cannot help here, but instead new, inner powers must be activated. Significant souls who are soon to work upon earth must be offered quite differently formed vessels of embodiment. Where young women develop a new type of spiritual-scientific self-education this will allow for the pre-birth education of future generations who will thus be equipped with new spiritual powers of knowledge and perception. Such powers will be indispensable to cope with severe suffering and trials in the future.

All harmful influences from the soft earth can be forcefully opposed and resisted with help from what one must call the *Immanuel-impulse*. The name means 'God in the midst of us' and (in Matthew, Chapter 1) points to spiritual forces of regeneration, and thus to eugenic occultism[53] which Rudolf Steiner predicted for the East. What in Christ's time related solely to the unique virginal birth of the Redeemer through Maria-Sophia aims gradually to become a shared human capacity in the new Christ era. The advent of eugenic occultism is imminent. Through it the Immanuel-impulse can work on earth from the etheric heights where Christ reigns.

III

Not only are healthy drives and life impulses at risk of corruption, but also feelings and emotions. We often pass by the glories of nature with indifference, and respond in an impoverished way to the souls of our fellow human beings. We remain cold to the highest truths. Who still feels reverence before what is holiest and noblest? Who still knows the inmost devotion of faith?

But in the path of knowledge set forth in *Theosophy* Rudolf Steiner showed that the persistent practice of feelings of selfless devotion and reverence transform our soul forces, cleanse our sympathies and antipathies so as to make them organs of perception for the supersensible. Instead of dull indifference we experience equanimity; instead of personal preference, open-souled warmth of heart; instead of lack of interest, devoted enthusiasm. These are the paths to the Grail Castle! Richard Wagner summed up the quality of those called to seek the Grail as 'Knowledge through compassion, the pure fool', in other words: being compassionate, open-minded and unprejudiced.

The Christ-bearer, the Redeemer, gave us the highest example of this. If we view the Grail chalice as a symbol then we can recognize that the Grail Being was the highest exemplar of soul devotion and the power of faith, consecrating himself wholly to a higher power. For that very reason he was able to become a vessel for the holy sun-blood of the Christ Spirit.

Anyone unable to be filled with the most inward feelings of adoration for what is holiest will never understand the Grail, for he is untouched by its flow of strength. Anyone, though, who cleanses his emotions in the sense of a 'disciple of Christ' is already linking himself with the 'new Grail-impulse' and can contribute a great deal to the healing of the steam earth (third subterranean layer) which corrupts all sentient and feeling life. Such a one lives wholly in the sense of the third Beatitude: 'Blessed are the meek, for they shall inherit the earth.'

The Grail-impulse is, at the same time, one of the five sources of inspiration of anthroposophy. The author has described these and their organic context in another work.[54]

IV

Only when embodied in physical human form and surrounded by the things of the senses does the soul come to self-awareness and develop a capacity for freedom. The form of the physical body is both an image and a tool of the thinking 'I' or ego, and the core form of all mineral things. The human being forms the latter into machines, but in doing so he is at risk of becoming the slave of technology. Advancing mechanization is leading to extensive replacement of human work and spirit by automata that are really anti-human. In this way the form earth (fourth chthonic layer) allows negative images of all physical things to arise through the thinking human being. As these mechanisms work back upon the human soul, its function of freedom is deadened and destroyed. Culture is dehumanized.

The *spiritual impulse of the new freedom* can counter this. One can draw this from the first realm of spirit, since it is there that the influx of the Atma ego from the seventh spirit-realm can be experienced. This comes to expression in the human experience of being 'a spirit among spirits, a part of the primal spirits; I feel in myself the Vedanta truth: I am the primal spirit' (Brahma, God).[55]

This fourth impulse will combat the threat of soullessness caused by radical mechanization, for through this awareness the ego capable of freedom can draw new strength.

But religious communities will call this impulse for freedom an 'unholy' one. And, used one-sidedly, it can indeed lead us into luciferic aberrations due to arrogant feelings of union with God. Therefore, Christ's admonition about moderation applies here: 'Blessed are those who hunger and thirst after righteousness.'

V

For community life in the future the following is a decisive truth: since Christ has been working in the etheric sphere, he also reigns as Lord of karmic connections. This deed not only blesses the earth's etheric mantle, but also the archetypal spiritual sphere where the laws of all living things are created by the wisdom that integrates each individual life into wholeness and harmony. Into this sphere works also the sixth realm of spirit-land, in which the human being's Life Spirit has its existence, containing in itself the totality of incarnation tasks set by God.

With regard to the new Christ era, we should try, already while on the earth, to shape our community life and mutual destinies in accordance with the laws at work in the second spirit-realm. Rudolf Steiner said of it, among other things, that 'human beings learn from experience that their individual destiny should not be separated from the community in which they live'. Here the decisive point is the living unity and harmony of the whole. The Pauline phrase can be illuminating here which speaks of how each person should carry the burdens of the other, and take on another's destiny as his own. Rudolf Steiner put it like this:

> The law of karma does not say that each person must bear the consequences of his own actions, but rather that the consequences of such actions must be borne, irrespective of who carries them. Just as here in physical life a brother or friend can take on something for another, so in a much deeper sense this can happen in the spiritual world, too.

It is time to develop the will for karmic solidarity! After all, we do not just have personal soul obligations to each other, but are also linked to one another in a spiritual-historical and karmic way. In our Life Spirit lives the duty, from one incarnation to the next, to work together with others to fulfil the superpersonal spiritual tasks which the Divine Sophia wrote into our names, so that each can contribute what he is able to the evolution of the whole of humanity. This knowledge increasingly asks us to try to give mutual assistance and to help carry the destinies of our fellow human beings in the name of Christ.[56]

This kind of mutual willingness to be there for and to serve one another will gradually become easier for those who try meditatively to imbue themselves with the fifth spiritual impulse, which bears the name the *New Revelation of Christ*.

Resulting from this, the strength of the Immanuel-impulse will flow towards humanity out of the etheric world. Through the fifth impulse one gains a vivid understanding of the obligations arising for the coexistence of free spirits from the truth that, henceforth, Christ has also become the Lord of Karma!

Embodying this impulse will have a healing influence on the dangerous emanations of the fruit earth (the fifth layer). With its unbounded, dispersing expansion tendency it is related to the life-corrupting soft earth (the second layer). The mushroom-like multiplying tendency of its rampant growth energy reminds one directly of cancer tumours or the life-destroying 'life' of micro-fungi and bacteria, in which individual life asserts itself without any consideration of its fellow creatures. The opposite of harmonious, holistic growth results: the death of the entire organism.

Let us not behave like bacilli to each other in the way we perceive each other's destinies. In history's new foundations of life and destiny, in the spirit of Christ, all human beings can find and live out their shared involvement and community with each other. To do so they need only see that their individual destiny is part of the spiritual tasks in life that must be completed together, whose higher, thematic unity is discernible in the Life Spirit.

The fifth Beatitude also urges us to practise loving compassion for each other. At the same time it expresses the fact that any progress of the whole always works back onto each developing individual: 'Blessed are the merciful, for they shall obtain mercy.'

VI

Those who purify their passions and desires and direct them selflessly towards the spirit are few in number. But since there are all too many whose unharnessed drives stir and whip up the fire earth (passion earth) of the sixth layer, we should expect dire earthquakes and volcanic catastrophes before long. Of that layer Rudolf Steiner commented:

> There is a connection between human passion and the passion substance of this layer. If human beings become very angry, for example, their anger intensifies this passion substance; that is what happened at the end of the Lemurian period. Through their passions the Lemurians made the fire earth rebellious and in this way they destroyed the whole Lemurian continent![57]

At that time, too, the earth was in a transitionary period from a Piscean Age to an Aquarian Age. Will we in future summon up our own and the earth's destruction through Ahriman?

Christ's answer from the apocalyptic future is: 'Behold, I make all things new.' The 21st chapter of the Revelation of St John speaks of a new earth and new heavenly spheres that will arise. Now when everything old is threatened with destruction, the Christ-impulse, taken up and furthered by human beings, begins to develop a new world from a spiritual seed force to fundamentally recreate humanity.

The creation of the earth and humanity began in the very ancient spiritual sphere of Saturn through the Father's divine will forces, while the creation of the physical human being started in the Lemurian epoch. But we should remember that in the third region of spirit-land (the Saturn sphere), where the archetypal images of all soul forces are creatively active, impulses from the fifth region also play in. That is the sphere of the eternal creative intentions and aims of the gods. It is for this very reason that the third spirit region (the Saturn sphere) is where the karmic decisions about human destiny are made.

From the realm of the karma powers, Ahriman's strength in the fire earth can be overcome and transformed.

The same divine creativity is nowadays inaugurating the re-creation of humanity, because Christ gives the karma powers the impulse for this transformation. *The new world beginning has already started.* In the midst of processes of decline the re-creation of the earth is beginning. All of the cosmic past conceals certain karmic seeds for corresponding future events, seeds of what can and should grow out of the earth and humanity. What is possible will then take shape as reality in accordance with the way the Christ gives impetus to these transformations.[58]

All those can help advance this noble aim of humanity's re-creation who unite themselves with an impulse which one can call the *impulse of re-creation.* Because the word 'renewal' is too weak for what is meant, one really needs to coin a new word altogether, such as 're-origination', with the meaning of *newly creating out of the archetype.* This 're-origination' impulse derives from the third spirit-realm, which is penetrated with the strength of the fifth sphere, the Saturn region of karma powers which, however, is nowadays encompassed by the all-transformative Christ.

Souls who, due to their willingness for sacrifice and their purity of heart, are capable of experiencing the blessedness of the third spirit region, are no doubt called first and foremost to serve this re-creation. Rudolf Steiner characterized such human beings as 'the great benefactors of the human race, devoted natures who perform great services within communities'. They acquired their capacity for this in the same region, after gaining a special relationship with it in former lives. The archetypal strength of such noble souls can be called upon repeatedly to help the process of re-creation and re-origination.

Being permeated by this impulse will bear fruit for human souls in the form of a new consciousness of all the archetypal ideals that emanate from the all-transformative Christ at ever higher stages of knowledge.

VII

Just as all spiritual powers of the heavenly spheres have their opposite numbers in the form of the adversarial powers of the Abyss, so the highest being of all, the Deus Absolutus, has a corresponding being at the core of the earth, named Lucifer by Dante and Deus Inversus or the Reversed God by the Rosicrucians. One could also speak of the Anti-Logos, if one understands the Logos to be the Lord of all divine powers. From the core of the earth the Reversed God works on humanity through all the spheres of evil to destroy it with their help. He becomes particularly active through the seventh layer of earth, where Ahriman works as 'earth mirror' or 'prism', sowing confusion in all trains of thought. Thus he is the adversary of the sphere of divine cosmic connections, the fourth region of spirit-land, where the I or ego originates as thought being. There, exercising the faculty of Inspiration, the meditant can hear the pattern of all God's cosmic ideas, as the harmony of archetypal images together creating cosmic sense and purpose—as Logos, or Word. Epistemology or logic is only a pale reflection of this.

But Ahriman plays a part in Creation. He distorts much of nature's spirit into counter-phenomena (e.g. by turning etheric light into electricity) and misleads human thinking into erroneous interpretations (for example, that electricity is the world soul). Numerous errors of thinking and categorization come about as a result of ahrimanic arts of illusion and distortion, for instance: the shifting of problems to realms where they do not belong; false analyses and syntheses; erroneous conclusions, etc. Everywhere his false reflections act as diversionary tactics to confuse practical thinking.

Our powers of thinking require great illumination to decipher the chaos of ideas which causes so much harm. Such inspired illumination comes to us from the seventh spiritual impulse, for which we have no name. Rudolf Steiner may owe a very great deal to this source of light, for his thought remained in harmony with the divine world order. In consequence, he was able to establish a 'knowledge that is in accordance with reality', whose intrinsic nature, as the methodological core of Anthropo-Sophia, he often described in the following way:

Thus, the essence of a thing only becomes apparent if it is brought into relationship with the human being, for only in the latter does the intrinsic nature of each thing appear.

Or in his autobiography:

The whole world, apart from the human being, is a riddle, the real riddle of existence, and the human being himself is its solution. But by saying this one also experiences the idea that in the world and its life, the Logos, wisdom itself, the Word holds sway.[59]

The human being's task is to use the perceiving and comprehending ego—through the strength of Christ—to fulfil the world creation process. Knowledge that accords with reality creates the seeds to form creation anew. Science has a universally important role here, for it concludes the work of creation. From spiritual seeds the newly created earth will manifest in the Jupiter planetary condition.

All-embracing knowledge through the power of the Logos, which reconciles all aspects of world thought in universal truth, leads to the Heavenly City of Peace with its twelve gates. As seer, Rudolf Steiner made the words of Christ a reality: 'Blessed are the peacemakers, for they shall be called the children of God.' These are words that apply to the ego-endowed human being of the consciousness soul who will give birth to the Spirit Self.

VIII

The fully mature consciousness soul bears the Spirit Self within it, which is why the culture of the Spirit Self is already germinating today. The spiritual impulse that works towards this is, therefore, of decisive importance. In the sixth letter to the Church at Philadelphia (meaning 'community of fraternal love'), the Revelation of St John describes the cultural conditions in which it will be realized.

The home of the Spirit Self is the fifth region of spirit-land, the realm of karma-determining world order. The Spirit Self is the bearer of karma. Its nature is substantially determined by the spiritual tasks implanted in it in accordance with the Sophia's plan of world evolution, as an overall task to be fulfilled through all incarnations in harmony with the 'aims and intentions' of the Godhead.

Due to common, shared qualities or similarities between those original tasks, spiritual families of destiny arose in movements and their metamorphoses throughout world history. The intention from above was for fraternal collaboration of human spirits in the service of God's spiritual aims. Spiritual brotherhoods were to form in freedom for this purpose and, by so doing, eventually the most varied spiritual orientations will come together as 'inhabitants' of the twelve-gated City of Peace, the *New Jerusalem*. That is why this name is inscribed into all the human names called to form this all-embracing fraternity. That is why the spiritual impulse that works to counter and heal the eighth level of the earth's interior, the fragmenter or splintering earth, is called the *Impulse of the New Jerusalem*. Elsewhere I have outlined[60] how this impulse has worked through long ages of cultural history. This relates to the ideal which Rudolf Steiner once characterized as follows: 'The evolution of humanity towards love and brotherhood is a continual overcoming of this eighth sphere.'

This all-embracing fraternity in Christ can only be achieved very gradually and through a great diversity of forms and manifestations. The ultimate goal is the community of all spiritual communities in the universal Christ. (Revelation, Chapter 7.)

The primal seed of this was formed by the church of Christ with its foundation stones, the twelve apostles. Throughout all ages and civilizations ever new, higher and more advanced forms of community must arise. Russian men of wisdom, such as Dostoyevsky and Soloviev, had some inkling of the future form of the Ecclesia. They spoke of a universal humanity, united in the Sophia, which is to form the bodily organism of Christ on earth. For the sixth cultural epoch a truly Christian human community, or Ecclesia, is trying to form anew, through the power of the maturing Jerusalem-impulse. The spiritual, cosmic human Self will be the uniting force, filled with the power of light and the fire of love, as Jacob Böhme described the Manas Being.

Here belongs the insight that the divine Sophia Being is one of the most important sources of inspiration of anthroposophy. And then we can reflect on what Rudolf Steiner said of the eighth sub-earthly sphere:

Human beings must work together in harmony to overcome the fragmenting power of the eighth level. This power

was implanted in the earth so that human beings themselves can develop harmony. The substance of all evil is
prepared and organized here. Quarrelsome people have a
particular relationship to this level and are influenced by it.
The strife between the two brothers Cain and Abel had its
source there. Thus this level brought the substance of evil
into the world.[61]

The healing counter-force, the impulse of the New Jerusalem,
must be drawn from the sphere of karmic destiny. It is
essential that today, when we are beginning to understand the
laws of karma, reconciliation and harmonious collaboration
can be achieved with individuals and karmic groups who, due
to ancient karma, have found their way into historical
movements that work in mutual opposition. The most
important of these world-historical and karmic oppositions
originated from Cain and Abel. What enormous significance
for the pending transformation of the eighth layer is the truth
that may be expressed thus: the conflict between Cain and
Abel has now been reconciled through the new Christ-
impulse, aided by the forces of karma!

Truly, Christ already holds sway now as Lord and trans-
former of karma!

The impulse of the New Jerusalem must fill human hearts
so that reconciliation from the heavenly spheres also works
into human beings on earth!

IX

One can only speak in veiled hints about the core of the earth
and the ninth spiritual impulse. We have no names to characterize either.

Spiritual science ultimately leads to practical occultism in three ways, via the health-giving (seventh) impulse, the eugenic (second) impulse and the mechanical (ninth) impulse. But the Abyss opposes each of the good ones with an evil one.

Some of today's technological inventions border on the magical. The sciences are fast becoming 'occult sciences'. In future they will increasingly be inspired from the depths, for certain, but also from the heights.

We are at the threshold of unimaginable advances. Initially the inventions that serve destruction always push themselves forward. But from the highest spiritual impulse will derive inventions that further human evolution and wrest from the anticipated metamorphoses of earthly life new life conditions for plants, animals and human beings.

Everything negative of this kind is the karmic consequence of the betrayed Vulcan Mysteries of Atlantis. These were founded by those who had fallen most strongly under Lucifer's influence, so that they were most awakened to individual thinking. They laid the foundations for the later sciences and arts. These original inventors were the Cain types (Genesis, Chapter 4). The word 'Cain' itself means 'individual thinker' or 'expert' and is concealed in the name of the underworld god of smiths: Vulcan, who is really called 'Vul-Cain'.

In future times—thanks to the ninth spiritual impulse— transformed Cain souls will be able to redeem the bad karma of the betrayed Vulcan Mysteries through highly benevolent inventions. In positive mechanical occultism new Vulcan Mysteries will arise, no doubt also supported, much later, by white magic working against the black magic of the earth core.

Ultimately even the Deus Inversus, or Lucifer, at the earth's core will be redeemed. By this means the perfection of the earth, the most highly spiritual Vulcan condition, can be prepared, where all physical existence will be transfigured into Atma-being.

But for long earth periods to come a developing opposition to Christ will harass and persecute spiritually advancing humanity with all the forces of evil. This will fulfil the Manichaean principle, however. Christ's ninth Beatitude will bring comfort here: 'Blessed are they who are persecuted for righteousness' sake, for theirs is the Kingdom of Heaven. Blessed are ye, when men shall revile you, and persecute you, and shall say all manner of evil against you falsely, for my sake.'

Notes

1. By Temple Lodge Publishing.
2. Rudolf Steiner, *Anthroposophical Leading Thoughts*, Rudolf Steiner Press, London 1973.
3. Ibid.
4. Nanotechnology comprises any technological developments on the nanometre scale, usually 0.1 to 100 nanometres. One nanometre equals one thousandth of a micrometre, or one millionth of a millimetre. It involves miniaturization to the atomic level and has relevance especially in the field of modern computer electronics.
5. Ray Kurzweil, *The Age of Spiritual Machines: When Computers Exceed Human Intelligence*, Penguin Books, New York 1999, p. 25.
6. Ibid, 41.
7. For more on 'supermaterialism' see Sergei Prokofieff's *The Spiritual Origins of Eastern Europe and the Future Mysteries of the Holy Grail*, Temple Lodge Publishing, London 1993, p. 285.
8. David F. Noble, *Forces of Production*, Alfred A. Knopf, New York 1984, p. xi, cited by Sheldon Krimsky in the Preface to his *Biotechnics and Society: The Rise of Industrial Genetics*, Praeger, New York 1991, p. xi.
9. Rudolf Steiner: *The Inner Realities of Evolution*, Rudolf Steiner Pub. Co., London 1953, Lecture 3, pp. 48–9.
10. *Blätter für Anthroposophie*, nos. 6, 7/8 and 9 (June to September).
11. Temple Lodge Publishing, London 1997.
12. Ibid.
13. Rudolf Steiner died on 30 March 1925.
14. Rudolf Steiner, *The Michael Mystery*, Anthroposophical Publishing Company, London 1956. Essay 19 is dated 'March

1925'. Also published as *Anthroposophical Leading Thoughts*, Rudolf Steiner Press, London 1973.

15. This word refers to members of the Anthroposophical Society.
16. Rudolf Steiner, *The Michael Mystery*, Anthroposophical Pub. Co., New York 1930.
17. Ibid.
18. Ibid.
19. Ibid.
20. Translator's note: this word, which recurs elsewhere, could be misconstrued in English. It in fact means a realm *above* natural laws (the original meaning of 'supernatural') rather than superlatively natural.
21. Rudolf Steiner, *The Michael Mystery*, Anthroposophical Pub. Co., New York 1930.
22. Ibid.
23. Ibid.
24. Ibid.
25. Plato's *Phaedo*, a dialogue that principally recounts the death of Socrates.
26. Rudolf Steiner, lecture of 31 July 1916, published as Lecture 3 in the cycle *The Riddle of Humanity*, Rudolf Steiner Press, London 1990. GA 170.
27. Ibid.
28. The Epistle of St Paul the Apostle to the Ephesians 6:11–13.
29. Ibid. 2:2 '... wherein once you walked according to the fashion of this world, according to the Prince of the power of the air about us, the Prince of the Spirit which now works on the unbelievers...'
30. Rudolf Steiner, lecture of 4 September 1906, 'Rosicrucian Training. The Interior of the Earth. Earthquakes and Volcanoes', published as Lecture 14 in the cycle *Founding a Science of the Spirit*, Rudolf Steiner Press, London 1999. GA 95.
31. Rudolf Steiner, lecture of 21 April 1906, 'The Interior of the Earth' (Das Innere der Erde) contained in the cycle *Das*

christliche Mysterium (The Christian Mystery) Rudolf Steiner Verlag, Dornach 1998. GA 97. Not translated into English.

32. Garber Communications, New York 1987. GA 94.

33. Rudolf Steiner, lecture of 1 January 1909, 'Mephistopheles and Earthquakes', published as Lecture 2 in the pamphlet *The Deed of Christ and the Opposing Spiritual Powers*, Rudolf Steiner Publishing Co., London 1954.

34. Adolf Arenson, Rudolf Steiner Publishing Co., London 1944 and Anthroposophic Press, New York 1944.

35. Currently measured at 6378.1 km equatorial radius; 6356.8 km polar radius.

36. *Natur und Idee*, Vienna 1861.

37. Rudolf Steiner, lecture of 4 September 1906, published as Lecture 14 in *Founding a Science of the Spirit*, Rudolf Steiner Press, London 1999.

38. S. Günther, *Handbuch der Geophysik*; Carl Ritter, *Die Erdkunde im Verhältnis zur Natur und zur Geschichte des Menschen*.

39. Adolf Arenson, op. cit. Translator's note: Arenson puts the first two sentences of the above in quotes and indicates in his text that the source of this 'law' is Rudolf Steiner.

40. 'Let no one deceive you in any way, for the day of the Lord will not come unless the apostasy comes first, and the man of sin is revealed, the son of perdition who opposes and is exalted above all that is called God, or who is worshipped, so that he sits in the temple of God and gives himself out as if he were God ... For the mystery of evil is already at work ...' 2 Thessalonians 2:3–7.

41. 'But know this, that in the last days dangerous times will come. Men will be lovers of self, covetous, haughty, proud, blasphemers, disobedient to parents, ungrateful, criminal, heartless, faithless, slanderers, incontinent, merciless, unkind, treacherous, stubborn, puffed up with pride, loving pleasure more than God, having a semblance indeed of piety, but disowning its power.' 2 Timothy 3:1–5.

42. Translator's note.

43. Translator's note.
44. Arenson, op. cit.
45. Translator's note.
46. Dante, *The Inferno*, 32nd Canto.
47. For a description of the centre of the earth since the Mystery of Golgotha, see Adalbert Graf von Keyserlingk, *The Birth of a New Agriculture*, Temple Lodge Publishing, London 1999. See pp. 84–6. '...at the moment when Christ's blood flowed down onto the earth at Golgotha a new sun-globe was born in the earth's interior'. Rudolf Steiner is quoted there as saying: 'The interior of the earth is of gold ... if one passes through them [the subterranean spheres] accompanied by Christ, the demons will not be able to harm you—but otherwise they would indeed be able to destroy you! They can, however, become our helpers. Yes, that is so—the path is a true one, but it is very difficult!'
48. Rudolf Steiner, lecture of 1 January 1909, published Lecture 14 in *Founding a Science of the Spirit*, Rudolf Steiner Press, London 1999.
49. *The Life of Jesus Christ and Biblical Revelations: From the Visions of the Venerable Anne Catherine Emmerich as recorded in the Journals of Clemens Brentano*, Tan Books and Publishers, Inc., Rockford, Illinois 1986, pp. 353–4.
50. Cf. also Revelations 9, 10; also Emil Bock's book, *The Apocalypse of Saint John*, Floris Books, Edinburgh.
51. This booklet was first published in 1953.
52. Referring to Jehovah as one of the Elohim.
53. Translator's note: This word does not, of course, mean any kind of direct physical/biological intervention in human DNA, but is a purely spiritual process of transformation and improvement with gradual effects on the physical body.
54. S. von Gleich, *The Sources of Inspiration of Anthroposophy*, Temple Lodge, London 1997.
55. Cf. Rudolf Steiner's *Theosophy*, Rudolf Steiner Press, London 1973.

56. Cf. Arenson's lecture, and the Stuttgart *Mitteilungen*, 1953, vol. 22 ff.
57. Rudolf Steiner, lecture of 4 September 1906, published in *Founding a Science of the Spirit*, Rudolf Steiner Press, London 1999.
58. Cf. Rudolf Steiner, *Occult Science—an Outline*, Rudolf Steiner Press, London 1979.
59. Rudolf Steiner, *Autobiography*, Anthroposophic Press, New York 1999.
60. St John's issue of the Stuttgart *Mitteilungen*, no. 22.
61. Rudolf Steiner, lecture of 4 September 1906.

Bibliography

Arenson, Adolf, *Das Erdinnere*, Freiburg 1980 (Series: 'Ergebnisse aus dem Studium der Geisteswissenschaft Rudolf Steiner's, vol. 2)

Bock, Emil, *Apokalypse. Betrachtungen über die Offenbarung des Johannes*, Stuttgart 1982

Braun, Emil, *Griechische Götterlehre*, Heidelberg 1859

Carus, Carl Gustav, *Natur und Idee oder das Werdende und sein Gesetz*, Vienna 1861

Emmerich, Anna Katharina, *Das Leben unsers Herrn und Heilandes Jesu Christi*, ed. Clemens Brentano 1858. New edition Aschaffenburg 1956

Gleich, Clemens von, 'Een teken aan de hemel—een teken aan de wand' (I. De komeet Halley in het verleden, II. Toekomstperspectieven). In: *Mededelingen van de Anthroposophie Vereniging in Nederland*, 1983, pp. 199, 232

Gleich, Sigismund von, *De Heilige graal en de nieuwe tijd van Christus*, Zeist 1952

—'Die überpersönliche Lebensbestimmung.' In: *Mitteilungen aus der anthroposophischen Arbeit in Deutschland*, no. 22 (1952)

—*The Sources of Inspiration of Anthroposophy*, Temple Lodge Publishing, London 1999.

Günther, Siegmund, *Handbuch der Geophysik*, Stuttgart 1897–9

Hesiod, *Theogony*

Ritter, Carl, *Die Erdkunde im Verhältnis zur Natur und zur Geschichte des Menschen*, Berlin 1817–18

Schuré, Edouard, *Esquisse d'une cosmogonie psychologique*, Paris 1928

Steiner, Rudolf, *Gesamtausgabe* (GA—complete edition), Dornach

—*Anthroposophical Leading Thoughts* (GA 26), London 1973

—*The Christian Mystery* (GA 97), Gympie 2000, lecture of 21 April 1906

—*Occult Science—an Outline* (GA 13), London 1979

—*True and False Paths of Spiritual Investigation* (GA 243), London 1985

—*Autobiography*, New York 1999 (GA 28)

—*The Riddle of Humanity* (GA 170), London 1990

—*Founding a Science of the Spirit* (GA 95), London 1999

Lectures by Rudolf Steiner relating to volcanic eruptions and earthquakes: 16 April 1906 (in GA 96); 12 June 1906 (in GA 94); 4 September 1906 (in GA 95); 1 Jan 1909 (in GA 107); 22 May 1910 (in GA 120); 26 November 1922 (in GA 219); 2 and 25 June 1923 (in GA 350); 27 and 29 June 1924 (in GA 236).